LinkedIn Profile and Resume Power Phrases

By Amanda Symonds

Introduction

Your LinkedIn profile and resume are both extremely important tools for your career and you should know how to optimise them for your job search. You need to include power verbs and phrases to attract attention from recruiters or headhunters and get to the interview stage and onto better jobs roles. We have included 500 power verbs and phrases suitable for time-poor professionals plus with our tips for writing a LinkedIn profile, cover letter and resume.

Please remember to leave a review online about your job search and help others find this book.

What to Optimize When Writing a LinkedIn Profile

1. Start with a strong headline that accurately describes your professional brand. Always make sure it is up to date and not in conflict with the current role you are applying for!

2. Use keyword-rich descriptions of your skills and experience using the verbs and phrases in this book.

3. Use industry jargon if it is relevant to the position you are targeting.

4. Highlight your accomplishments and use concrete examples wherever possible.

5. Use strong action verbs to describe your professional achievements.

6. Keep your profile updated with your current contact information. Update your current role.

7. Use a professional-looking headshot as your profile picture. So many recruiters will search for you on LinkedIn to see your picture and check whether your profile
 matches your resume.

8. Choose a simple and professional layout for your profile. Use an LinkedIn Banner image from Canva to stand out.

9. Customize your URL to include your name or keywords for your brand.

10. Look at other professional's profiles then you connect to them and think about what you could improve.

11. Use formal language throughout your profile.

12. Edit your profile thoroughly before publishing it.

13. Include links to your website or blog, if relevant.

14. Connect with people you know and request recommendations from past employers or colleagues. Recruiters will read them. Try to get a great recommendation for each role you have listed.

15. Join relevant groups and participate in discussions to build your credibility.

16. Regularly update your profile with new information about your professional brand. These updates may be read by recruiters or headhunters.

17. Use keywords from the job listing in your profile to get found by recruiters searching LinkedIn.

18. Highlight your skills and experience that match the job requirements.

19. Make sure you check your messages every 2 days when job hunting.

20. Always follow up after connecting with someone on LinkedIn. Send a personalized message and mention something you have in common or why you are reaching out.

By following these tips, you can create a LinkedIn profile that will stand out from the rest.

LinkedIn Phrases with Gaps

1. "I am a X professional with X years of experience."

2. "I have a proven track record in X."

3. "I am passionate about X."

4. "I have a strong interest in X."

5. "I am a motivated self-starter who is always looking for new challenges."

6. "I thrive in fast-paced environments and enjoy working on multiple projects at once."

7. "I am an excellent communicator, both written and verbally."

8. "I have superb organizational skills and can always keep things running smoothly."

9. "I'm known for my attention to detail and my ability to catch even the smallest errors."

10. "I'm a quick learner and always eager to take on new tasks."

11. "I have a deep understanding of X."

12. "I am an expert in X."

13. "I have a strong background in X."

14. "I am well-versed in X."

15. "I have extensive experience with X."

16. "My skills include X, Y, and Z."

17. "In my previous role, I was responsible for X"

18. "I successfully completed X projects while working at Y."

19. "I have received numerous awards and accolades for my work in X."

20. "I am often consulted by my colleagues for my X expertise."

Power Verbs for your LinkedIn Profile and Resume

1. Accelerated

2. Achieved

3. Administered

4. Analyzed

5. Assessed

6. Authored

7. Boosted

8. Chaired

9. Consolidated

10. Coordinated

11. Created

12. Delegated

13. Designed

14. Developed

15. Directed

16. Enhanced

17. Evaluated

18. Executed

19. Expedited

20. Facilitated

21. Formulated

22 . Fostered

23. Generated

24. Guided

25. Implemented

26. Improved

27. Incorporated

28. Inspected

29. Instituted

30. Led

31. Maintained

32. Managed

33. Monitored

33. Motivated

34. Negotiated

35. Operated

36. Overhauled

37. Oversaw

38. Planned

39. Presented

40. Prioritized

41. Processed

42. Promoted

43. Prosecuted

44. Provided

45. Recommended

46. Reconciled

47. Recruited

48. Reorganized

49. Researched

50. Restructured

51. Reviewed

52. Revamped

53. Simplified

54. Solved

55. Spearheaded

56. Streamlined

57. Supervised

58. Supplemented

59. Supported

60. Taught

61. Trained

62. United

63. Upheld

64. Validated

65. Verified

66. Wrote

20 Bullet Point Examples for Responsibilities and Experience

- Handled all incoming customer inquiries via phone and email

- Managed customer accounts and updated account information as necessary

- Processed customer orders and tracked order status from start to finish

- Assisted with product returns and exchanges

- Provided recommendations for products and services that best fit customer needs

- Built strong relationships with customers to promote customer satisfaction and loyalty

- Resolved customer complaints in a professional and efficient manner

- Effectively communicated with other departments to resolve customer issues

- Maintained up-to-date knowledge of company products, services, and policies

- Documentation of all customer interactions in CRM software

- Consistently met or exceeded monthly sales goals

- Acted as a team leader in the absence of the department manager

- Assisted with training new customer service representatives

- Conducted quality assurance audits of customer service interactions

By following these tips, you can create a profile and resume that will stand out from the rest. We will jump forward to cover letter creation.

Top Tips to Remember When Writing a Cover Letter

1. Address the letter to the specific person who will be reading it.

2. Use a formal and professional tone.

3. Keep it short and to the point.

4. Highlight your relevant skills and experience.

5. Tailor your cover letter to each individual job you apply for.

6. Use strong action verbs to describe your accomplishments.

7. Use specific and concrete examples whenever possible.

8. Avoid using clichés or overused phrases.

9. Proofread your cover letter carefully before sending it.

10. Include all necessary contact information in your signature.

11. You can save your cover letter as a PDF to ensure proper formatting.

12. Address any questions or concerns the employer may have.

13. Reiterate your interest in the position and company.

14. Thank the employer for their time and consideration.

15. Choose a professional cover letter template and layout.

16. Use white space to make your cover letter more readable.

17. Keep your cover letter to one page in length.

18. Use formal language throughout your cover letter.

19. Edit your cover letter thoroughly before sending it.

20. Always send a cover letter with your resume
or job application.

Example Cover Letter

I would like to apply for the position of .. , you have advertised on <date> .

I am a X professional with Y years of experience. I have a proven track record in Z and I am passionate about A.
I am currently working remotely as a B for C , but I am interested in relocating to D to be closer to family. In my previous role, I was responsible for E . I successfully completed F projects while working at G .

I have received numerous awards and accolades for my work in H. I am often consulted by my colleagues for my I expertise. I am confident that I have the skills and experience required for this position and I would be a valuable asset to your team.

Please find attached my resume for your review. I look forward to hearing from you soon.

Thank you,

Sincerely,

Your name

Notes about ATS Resume Software

An ATS (Applicant Tracking System) is a software program used by employers to filter out job applicants who are not qualified for the position. Many larger companies use this type of software, so it's important to ensure that your resume is formatted correctly and includes all the relevant keywords and phrases that the ATS will be looking for.

Some tips for optimizing your resume for an ATS include:

1. Use a simple, clean layout with clear headings and bullet points.

2. Avoid using images, charts, or other graphics.

3. Use standard fonts that are easy to read, not rare fonts.

4. Include all relevant keywords and phrases from the job listing.

5. Avoid using abbreviations or acronyms.

6. Use industry-specific jargon if it is mentioned in the job description or criteria.

7. Proofread your resume carefully to avoid any typos or grammatical errors.

8. Save your resume as a PDF to ensure it keeps its original formatting.

9. Test your resume with an ATS resume scanner prior to applying for jobs.

With these tips in mind, you can improve your chances of having your resume pass through an ATS and land you an interview.

Our Advice When Writing a Resume

1. Tailor your resume to each individual job you apply for. Rewrite it to highlight the job description skills so the ATS software can score your resume highly.

2. Use a formal and professional tone.

3. Keep it short and to the point.

4. Highlight your relevant skills and experience, **rewrite it to highlight the job description skills.**

5. Use strong action verbs to describe your accomplishments.

6. Use specific and concrete examples whenever possible.

7. Avoid using clichés or overused phrases.

8. Proofread your resume carefully before sending it.

9. Include all necessary contact information in your signature.

10. You can save your resume as a PDF to ensure proper formatting.

11. Choose a professional resume template and layout.

12. Use white space to make your resume more readable.

13. Keep your resume to one page in length, if possible or two pages.

14. Use formal language throughout your resume.

15. Edit your resume thoroughly before sending it.

16. Use an ATS-friendly format and include keywords from the job listing.

17. Use industry jargon if it is relevant to the position you are applying for.

18. Highlight your skills and experience that match the job requirements.

19. Make sure your resume is updated with your current contact information. Pictures may not work in the ATS scanner.

20. Always follow up after submitting your resume. Create a spreadsheet with file numbers and dates. Enter your follow-up calls on the spreadsheet and who you spoke to. You will sound informed, interested and memorable - you may get an interview based on your ability to remember facts and names!

By following these tips, you can create a resume that will stand out from the rest.

Top Tips for Job Hunting after Maternity Leave or a Career Break

1. Get your resume and cover letter updated and professionally written, if necessary.

2. Start with an objective or summary statement that accurately reflects your skills, experience and goals.

3. Use breaks in time to add a section saying Maternity Leave with years.

4. Understand you may be expected to apply for part-time roles if the baby is younger than 12 months.

5. Use keywords related to your skills, experience and goals in your resume and cover letter.

6. Research the company culture before applying to ensure it is a good fit for your family. If not, look for another company.

7. Consider what schedule you are looking for - full-time, part-time, job share or flexible work from home?

8. Talk to your partner about your job search and what you are looking for in a role.

9. Utilize your network of friends, family and professionals to help you with your job search.

10. Join relevant LinkedIn groups and participate in discussions.

11. Attend relevant online industry events, meetups and webinars.

12. Follow companies you are interested in on social media.

13. Read articles related to your industry and job search to keep up-to-date.

14. Use an online tool like Jobscan to optimize your resume for Applicant Tracking Systems (ATS).

15. Consider using a Recruiter to help with your job search.

16. Be prepared for interviews by practising answers to common questions.

17. Ask a friend or family member to mock interview you.

18. Be honest about your career break in interviews and be prepared to talk about it.

19. Use a professional-looking headshot as your profile picture.

20. Connect with people you know and request recommendations from past employers or colleagues on LinkedIn. Recruiters will read them. Try to get a great recommendation for each role you have listed.

12 Simple Tips to Get Headhunted from Your LinkedIn Profile

Are you looking for a new job opportunity? Are you tired of applying online and never hearing back? If so, then you need to start focusing on your LinkedIn profile. A great way to get headhunted is to make sure your profile is optimized and standing out from the rest. In this blog post, we will discuss 11 simple tips that will help you get headhunted from your LinkedIn Profile!

Tip # 1

Your profile photo is the first thing recruiters will see when they come across your profile, so it's important to make a good impression. Choose a professional headshot that is cropped close to your head and shoulders. Check photos of other employees at your dream company and make sure your photo looks similar in style to those people. Truth hurts: I have had to use a photo of me in my 30s to get hired for my current role (as I am in my 40s).

Tip #2: Become a Linkedin "All-Star"

LinkedIn reports that a profile meeting these criteria receives approximately forty times the number of connections as one that does not.

The criteria for "All-Star" status is simple:

A Photo

A current and previous job role

At least 50 connections

A profile summary

Education information

A industry

A location

Make sure you get this done before moving to the next stage!

Tip # 3

Make sure your headline is catchy and attention-grabbing. Your headline should be a brief summary of who you are and what you do. Include keywords that are relevant to the types of positions you are interested in.

Tip # 4

In the About section of your profile, write a summary that tells recruiters what you have to offer. This is not the time to be modest – highlight your skills, experience, and accomplishments. Use keywords that are relevant to the types of positions you are interested in.

Tip # 5

In the Experience section of your profile, list your current and past jobs in reverse chronological order. For each job, include a brief description of your duties and responsibilities. Use keywords that are relevant to the types of positions you are interested in.

Tip # 6

In the Skills & Endorsements section of your profile, list any skills that would be relevant to the types of positions you are interested in. You can also ask friends or colleagues to endorse you for these skills.

Tip # 7

In the Education section of your profile, list any relevant degrees or certifications you have. If you're still in school, you can list your expected graduation date and degree program.

Tip # 8

In the Volunteer Experience & Causes section of your profile, list any relevant volunteer experience or causes you support. This is a great way to show recruiters that you're passionate about something outside of work.

Tip # 9

In the Interests section of your profile, list any hobbies or interests that would be relevant to the types of positions you are interested in. For example, if you're interested in a job in marketing, you could list interests such as social media, market research, and brand management.

Tip # 10

The Recommendations section of your profile is a great way to show off your skills and experience. Ask past employers, clients, or colleagues to write a recommendation for you.

Tip # 11

The Projects section of your profile is a great way to showcase any relevant side projects you've worked on. This is a good place to include information about personal projects, open source contributions, and anything else that would be relevant to the types of positions you are interested in.

Tip # 12

Joining groups will increase your visibility for several reasons. The most important of these is that when you signup, you become a 2nd-degree network or connection of everyone else. This is the fastest way, to grow your extended network and get more people viewing your profile. I'd encourage you to join the GatedTalent group on Linkedin, which will allow you to network with thousands of recruiters and senior-level executives.

By following these simple tips, you can make sure your LinkedIn profile is optimized and headhunters will be knocking down on your door with job opportunities! Stay tuned for our next blog post where we'll discuss how to use LinkedIn to find a job that's not posted online!

The Top 15 Roles for Remote Work Opportunities

If you're looking for a remote work opportunity, you're in luck! The remote work market is booming, and there are plenty of roles to consider. This includes roles in all industries, from marketing to programming. So whether you're a stay-at-home mom or dad looking for a new career path, or you just want to telecommute occasionally, there's sure to be a role here that's suitable for your experience! Here is our list of roles to consider:

Social Media Manager

Do you love spending time on social media? If so, then being a social media manager might be the perfect remote work opportunity for you! As a social media manager, you would be responsible for creating and managing social media accounts for businesses or organizations. This could include creating content, responding to comments and messages, and monitoring activity on the account.

Programmer

If you're a programmer who is looking for a remote work opportunity, there are plenty of options available to you as well. You could work as a web developer, designing and coding websites for clients. Or, you could work as a software developer, creating new applications and programs. There are also many remote positions available for database administrators and system analysts.

Marketer

There are also many remote work opportunities available for marketers. You could work as a content marketer, creating and managing online content for businesses. Or, you could work as a social media marketer, developing and implementing social media campaigns. And if you're interested in working in the field of email marketing, there are also many remote positions available.

Customer Service Representative

Are you interested in working in customer service? If so, then being a remote customer service representative might be the perfect job for you! As a remote customer service representative, you would be responsible for handling customer inquiries and complaints via phone, email, or chat.

Salesperson

Do you have experience in sales? If so, then being a remote salesperson might be the perfect job for you! As a remote salesperson, you would be responsible for generating leads and closing deals with customers. You could work in a variety of industries, such as technology, automotive, or real estate.

Virtual Assistant

A virtual assistant is another great option for those who are looking for a remote work opportunity. As a virtual assistant, you would provide administrative support to clients from all over the world. This could include tasks such as scheduling appointments, managing email accounts, and providing customer service.

Writer

Do you have experience in writing? If so, then being a remote writer might be the perfect job for you! There are many different types of writing jobs available, including content writing, copywriting, and technical writing. And if you're interested in working as an editor or proofreader, there are also many remote positions available.

Data Entry Specialist

If you're looking for a remote work opportunity that doesn't require much experience, then being a data entry specialist might be the perfect job for you! As a data entry specialist, you would be responsible for entering data into computer systems. This could include tasks such as transcribing medical records or updating customer information.

Web Designer

Are you creative and have experience in web design? If so, then being a remote web designer might be the perfect job for you! As a web designer, you would be responsible for creating and designing websites for clients. You would need to have a strong understanding of web development, as well as experience in using design software.

Project Manager

Are you organized and have experience in project management? If so, then being a remote project manager might be the perfect job for you! As a project manager, you would be responsible for overseeing the development of projects. This could include tasks such as creating timelines, assigning tasks to team members, and tracking progress.

Accountant

Do you have experience in accounting or bookkeeping? If so, then being a remote accountant might be the perfect job for you! As an accountant, you would be responsible for managing financial accounts for businesses or individuals. This could include tasks such as preparing tax returns, maintaining ledgers, and processing invoices.

Consultant

If you're an expert in your field and are looking for a remote work opportunity, then being a consultant might be the perfect job for you! As a consultant, you would provide advice and guidance to clients in your area of expertise. You could work in a variety of industries, such as healthcare, education, or business.

Mediator

After some online training, you could work as an online mediator, helping people resolve disputes without having to go to court. You'd need good people skills, the ability to stay calm in heated situations, and experience in mediation, arbitration or conflict resolution.

Translator

Do you speak more than one language fluently? If so, then being a remote translator might be the perfect job for you! As a translator, you would be responsible for translating documents or audio files from one language to another. You would need to have a strong understanding of both languages, as well as excellent writing skills.

Recruiter

If you're experienced in human resources and are looking for a remote work opportunity, then being a remote recruiter might be the perfect job for you! As a remote recruiter, you would be responsible for sourcing and hiring candidates for open positions. You would need to have a strong understanding of the job market, as well as experience in using recruiting software.

Agencies are the Easiest Way to Land a New Job

If you're looking for a new job, you know that it can be tough to find the right opportunity. It seems like everyone is competing for the same jobs, and it's hard to stand out from the crowd. If you're looking for an easy way to land a new job, consider using an agency to shortcut this process.

If you're looking for a new job, consider registering with several agencies. Here are several reasons why:

Agencies have relationships with some of the best companies in the industry. If you're looking to work with a specific company, agencies usually have good relationships with employers and may be able to help you get your foot in the door.

Agencies are always looking for talented professionals to be in their talent pool. If you have the skills and experience that an agency is looking for, they will be eager to hire you as one of their contractors.

You can use an agency's resources to your advantage. Agency staff members are usually well-connected and can help you find the right job opportunity.
An agency gets paid when you get hired. An agency's main priority is to get you hired so their services are free of charge until you do.
Therefore, they will do everything they can to

help you find a job through them, including redoing your resume.

An agency can help you negotiate your salary and benefits package. They want to make sure you're getting the best possible deal, so they will fight for you.

If you register with an agency for temporary contract work then they will be more likely to offer you a full-time job with that employer (or another in the same field) if they are impressed with your work. This is because they have already invested time and resources in you and they know your capabilities.

Even if you're not sure what kind of job you want, an agency will give you feedback on your current resume. This really shortcuts the job hunting process.

It is a good idea to check the reviews of several recruitment agencies for your industry and connect with recruiters who hire (for your industry and role) on LinkedIn.

Job Hunting Scams to Watch Out For in 2022

Job hunting can be a difficult process, and unfortunately, scammers take advantage of job seekers looking for work.

The first job hunting scam to watch out for is job postings that are too good to be true. These job postings may promise high salaries, remote working conditions, flexible hours or little to no experience required. If you come across a job posting like this, do your research before applying. You can start by searching for reviews of the company online, indeed.com can help you do this. Also, be sure to contact the company directly to ask about the job posting. If the company is not able to provide you with more information about the job, it is likely a scam.

Another common job hunting scam is when scammers pose as recruiters or hiring managers. They may reach out to you through LinkedIn first, then email or social media and offer you a job opportunity and even organise a fake interview with another scammer. You may be asked for your credit card information in order to book a meeting room for a second interview. This is where the scam starts.

However, they will often ask for personal information, such as your Social Security number or bank account information. They may also ask you to pay a fee to apply for the job or to secure the position. Do not respond to these requests! Legitimate recruiters and hiring managers will never ask for this type of information upfront. If you are unsure if a job offer is legitimate, do some research on the company and the person who contacted you. If the scammer (recruiter) does not use a company email address then they may not even work at the recruitment company.

For instance, a scammer may have a LinkedIn profile that looks great and has a great employment history in several reputable agencies. You need to check for RED flags! Some of these could be:

-They are not linked to other employees in the same recruitment company

-You have no shared connections with the recruiter even though you supposedly work in the same industry (IT, for example). You should have some shared connections if you have more than 200 connections on your profile. That means they might have a fake profile.

-They have no gold 'In' on the right hand side of their profile. All recruiters pay for LinkedIn Premium access to search for and contact potential candidates.

-They keep using their gmail or other account for job related emails when though they are supposed to be 'at work'.

Finally, be wary of job offer that require you to give money upfront. This is a common scam where job seekers are asked to pay a fee to apply for a job or to participate in an interview. These fees can range from a few dollars to hundreds of dollars. If you come across a job posting that requires payment, beware! You should never have to pay to apply for a job or participate in an interview.

Job hunting can be difficult, but there are ways to protect yourself from scammers. If you are ever unsure about a job offer or job posting, do your research! You can also contact the Better Business Bureau (bbb.org) to report any suspicious job offers.

20 Things to Remember During the Interview

1. First impressions matter, so dress the part.

2. Be on time, or even early.

3. Have a firm handshake.

4. Make eye contact and smile.

5. Speak clearly and confidently.

6. Avoid using filler words, such as "um" or "like."

7. Show that you're engaged by nodding your head and making appropriate comments.

8. Don't badmouth your current or former employer.

9. Be honest if you're asked about your weaknesses.

10. Ask thoughtful questions about the company and the role you're interviewing for.

11. Be aware of your body language.

12. Avoid fidgeting, slouching, or crossing your arms.

13. Take your time in answering questions.

14. Don't rush your answers or blurt out the first thing that comes to mind.

15. Be aware of the interviewer's body language.

16. If they seem bored or uninterested, try to liven up the conversation.

17. At the end of the interview, thank the interviewer for their time.

18. Follow up with a thank-you note or email within 24 hours of the interview.

19. If you're asked for additional information, such as a writing sample, provide it promptly.

20. If you're not interested in the role, politely decline any further interviews or communication.

Example Interview Questions and Answers

1. Tell me about yourself.

2. Why are you interested in this position?

3. What are your strengths?

4. What are your weaknesses?

5. Tell me about a time when you faced a challenge at work and how you dealt with it.

6. Tell me about a time when you had to go above and beyond your job duties.

7. Tell me about a time when you made a mistake at work and how you handled it.

8. Tell me about a time when you had to deal with a difficult customer or co-worker.

9. Tell me about a time when you had to meet a tight deadline.

10. Tell me about a time when you had to work with little or no supervision.

11. Tell me about a time when you had to deal with a stressful situation.

12. What are your career aspirations?

13. What are your salary expectations?

14. What is your availability?

15. What are your long-term career aspirations?

16. Tell me about a time when you had to make a decision under pressure.

17. Tell me about a time when you had to take on a leadership role.

18. What are your favorite and least favorite things about your current job?

19. Tell me about a time when you had to give feedback to a co-worker.

20. What are your strengths and weaknesses?

Thank You Letter Template

Dear _____,

Thank you so much for taking the time to interview me yesterday. I really appreciate it. I am confident that I have the skills and experience that you are looking for and would be a great addition to your team. I am looking forward to hearing from you soon.

Sincerely,

Your name

Power Phrases about Attention to Detail

1. "I have an eye for detail and I'm always catching errors that others miss."

2. "I take great pride in my work and I make sure that everything is always perfect."

3. "I'm known for being a bit of a perfectionist, but it pays off in the end."

4. "My attention to detail ensures that every project is done right the first time."

5. "I always go the extra mile to make sure that my work is of the highest quality."

6. "I have a track record of producing results that exceed expectations."

7. "I have a history of completing projects on time and under budget."

8. "My clients are always happy with the final product because I pay attention to every detail."

9. "I have a reputation for being a perfectionist, but it's because my clients expect the best."

10. "I always deliver quality work, no matter what the project or deadline."

Power Phrases about Accuracy

1. "I have a reputation for being extremely accurate in my work."

2. "I take great care to make sure that all of my work is error-free."

3. "I'm known for being a stickler for details, and it pays off in the accuracy of my work."

4. "I always double-check my work to make sure that everything is correct."

5. "I take pride in producing work that is error-free and meets all expectations."

6. "My attention to detail ensures that I always deliver accurate results."

7. "My clients can always count on me to deliver accurate and reliable information."

8. "You can trust that my work is always accurate and up to par."

9. "I'm known for being a reliable and accurate source of information."

10. "My clients always know that they can count on me to deliver accurate results."

Power Phrases about Analytical Skills

1. "I have a keen eye for detail and I'm always looking for patterns and trends."

2. "I'm excellent at spotting errors and discrepancies in data."

3. "I have a knack for finding the root cause of problems."

4. "I'm always analyzing data to look for ways to improve efficiency."

5. "I excel at finding creative solutions to complex problems."

6. "My analytical skills are superb, and I'm always coming up with new ideas."

7. "I'm known for being a creative thinker and an out-of-the-box problem solver."

8. "My clients always come to me when they need fresh ideas and innovative solutions."

9. "I have a reputation for being a creative thinker, and I'm always coming up with new ideas."

10. "I'm always looking for ways to improve efficiency and effectiveness."

Power Phrases about Attendance and Punctuality

1. "I have a perfect attendance record."

2. "I've never missed a day of work."

3. "I'm always on time for my shifts."

4. "I'm known for being a punctual and reliable employee."

5. "My clients can always count on me to be on time for appointments."

6. "I always make sure that I'm where I'm supposed to be"

7. "You can trust that I'll always be there when you need me."

8. "I take my commitments seriously, and I always show up on time."

9. "If I say I'll be there, you can count on it."

10. "I'm known for being a dependable and reliable employee."

Power Phrases about Attitude

1. "I'm always positive and upbeat, no matter what the situation."

2. "I have a can-do attitude and I'm always ready to take on new challenges."

3. "I'm known for being a team player and working well with others."

4. "I'm flexible and adaptable, and I'm always willing to try new things."

5. "My clients always appreciate my positive attitude and upbeat personality."

6. "I'm known for being a go-getter and not taking 'no' for an answer."

7. "I have a 'can do' attitude and I'm always up for a challenge."

8. "My positive attitude is contagious, and it always helps to motivate others."

9. "I'm known for being a cheerful and optimistic person."

10. "My clients always enjoy working with me because of my positive attitude."

Power Phrases about Business Budgeting

1. "I have a proven track record of being able to keep project spending within the approved limit in the budget."

2. "I'm excellent at finding ways to save money and reduce costs in the business."

3. "I have a keen eye for spotting wasteful spending in a budget."

4. "I'm always looking for ways to increase revenue and decrease expenses."

5. "My employers/clients always appreciate my ability to stay within their budget."

6. "I have a reputation for being a frugal and savvy business person."

7. "I know how to stretch a dollar, and I always get the most bang for my buck."

8. "My employers always know that they can count on me to save them money in their operations."

9. "I'm known for being a penny-pincher, but in a good way!"

10. "My clients always save money when they work with me."

Power Phrases about Business Development

1. "I'm always looking for ways to grow my business."

2. "I have a reputation for being a very successful business development professional."

3. "I'm known for being able to bring in new business ."

4. "I have a lot of experience in business development."

5. "I'm known for being able to cultivate new business relationships."

6. "My clients appreciate my ability to grow their businesses."

7. "I'm always looking for ways to increase my company's bottom line."

8. "I'm known for being a very results-oriented person."

9. "I always make sure that I'm focused on business development."

10. "My clients know that they can count on me to help them grow their businesses."

Power Phrases about Closing Skills

1. "I'm excellent at closing deals and making sales."

2. "I always go the extra mile to make sure that my clients are satisfied."

3. "I have a proven track record of being able to close deals and achieve goals."

4. "My employers/clients always appreciate my tenacity and drive to succeed."

5. "I'm known for being a go-getter and not taking 'no' for an answer."

6. "I'm always looking for ways to increase revenue and decrease expenses."

7. "My positive attitude is contagious, and it always helps to motivate others."

8. "I'm known for being a cheerful and optimistic person."

9. "My clients always enjoy working with me because of my positive attitude."

10. "I'm known for being a persuasive and convincing speaker."

Power Phrases about Cooperation

1. "I'm always willing to cooperate and work with others."

2. "I'm known for being a team player who is always willing to help out."

3. "I'm flexible and easy to work with, and I'm always open to new ideas."

4. "My clients appreciate my cooperative attitude and my willingness to work with them."

5. "I'm always looking for ways to improve communication and cooperation."

6. "I have a reputation for being a helpful and cooperative person."

7. "I'm known for being a good listener and taking others' needs into consideration."

8. "My clients always know that they can count on me to be a good team player."

9. "I'm always willing to lend a helping hand."

10. "I'm known for being a cooperative and supportive person."

Power Phrases about Communication Skills

1. "I have superb written and verbal communication skills."

2. "I'm an excellent listener, and I always make sure that I understand what people are saying."

3. "I'm known for being a great communicator, and I always make sure that I'm clear and concise."

4. "My clients always appreciate my clear and concise communication style."

5. "I'm always able to find the right words to say, no matter what the situation."

6. "I'm always able to get my point across clearly and effectively."

7. "I have a reputation for being an excellent communicator, both in writing and in person."

8. "I have a knack for putting people at ease, and I'm always able to build rapport quickly."

9. "I have a knack for diffusing tense situations with my calm and professional communication style."

10. "My clients always know that they can rely on me to keep them updated and informed."

Power Phrases about Conceptual Thinking

1. "I have a knack for seeing the big picture and understanding complex concepts."

2. "I'm always able to see things from different perspectives and find new ways to look at problems."

3. "I'm known for being a strategic thinker, and I'm always looking for ways to improve effectiveness."

4. "My clients always appreciate my ability to think strategically and see the big picture."

5. "I'm always able to find creative solutions by thinking outside the box."

6. "I have a reputation for being an innovative thinker, and I'm always coming up with new ideas."

7. "I'm known for being a quick learner who is able to understand complex concepts quickly."

8. "I have a proven track record of success in conceptualizing and executing innovative ideas."

9. "I'm always able to think on my feet and come up with creative solutions on the fly."

10. "My clients know that they can rely on me to provide creative and innovative ideas."

Power Phrases about Conflict Management

1. "I have a reputation for being a calming influence in tense situations."

2. "I'm always able to diffusing tense situations with my calm and professional demeanour."

3. "My clients always appreciate my ability to keep cool under pressure."

4. "I'm known for being a level-headed person who is able to stay calm in stressful situations."

5. "I have a proven track record of success in managing and resolving conflicts."

6. "I'm always able to find common ground and reach mutually acceptable resolutions."

7. "My clients know that they can count on me to mediate disputes in a fair and objective manner."

8. "I have a knack for seeing both sides of every issue, and I'm always able to find win-win solutions."

9. "I'm always able to find the middle ground and reach compromises that everyone can agree on."

10. "My clients know that they can rely on me to resolve conflicts in a constructive and amicable manner."

Power Phrases about Consulting Skills

1. "I have a reputation for being an excellent consultant, and I'm always able to provide valuable insights."

2. "My clients always appreciate my ability to help them see things from different perspectives."

3. "I'm known for being a trusted advisor who is always able to offer sound and objective advice."

4. "I have a proven track record of success in helping businesses achieve their goals."

5. "My clients know that they can count on me to provide honest and unbiased feedback."

6. "I'm always able to offer helpful and constructive criticism that leads to positive results."

7. "I'm known for being a candid and frank person, and my clients appreciate my honesty."

8. "I have a knack for seeing the potential in people and businesses, and I'm always able to help them reach their full potential."

9. "I'm always able to offer insightful and thought-provoking ideas that help my clients achieve their goals."

10. "My clients know that they can rely on me to provide sound and trusted advice that leads to success."

Power Phrases about Creativity

1. "I have a reputation for being a creative thinker, and I'm always coming up with new ideas."

2. "I'm always looking for ways to improve efficiency and effectiveness."

3. "I have a knack for thinking outside the box and coming up with creative solutions."

4. "My clients always appreciate my creative approach to problem-solving."

5. "I'm known for being a resourceful and innovative thinker."

6. "I'm always able to find creative ways to overcome obstacles."

7. "My clients know that they can count on me to come up with creative and original ideas."

8. "I have a proven track record of success in coming up with creative solutions ."

9. "I'm always able to think on my feet and come up with creative solutions on the fly."

10. "My clients know that they can rely on me to provide creative and innovative ideas."

Power Phrases about Customer Service Skills

1. "I have a knack for matching people with the perfect solution."

2. "I always go the extra mile to make sure that my clients are happy."

3. "I'm known for being patient and understanding, even in difficult situations."

4. "My clients always feel valued and appreciated when they work with me."

5. "I always take the time to really understand what my clients need."

6. "My clients are always my top priority, and I'm always looking for ways to improve their experience."

7. "I'm known for being a customer service expert, and I always go above and beyond to help my clients."

8. "I have a passion for helping others, and I always make sure that my clients are taken care of."

9. "My goal is always to provide the best possible customer experience."

10. "I'm committed to providing outstanding customer service, every time."

Power Phrases about Dependability

1. "My clients know that they can count on me to be there when they need me."

2. "I'm always available to my clients and I'm always quick to respond to their needs."

3. "I have a reputation for being a reliable and dependable person."

4. "I'm known for being someone who follows through on their commitments."

5. "I always make sure that my clients can rely on me to be there for them."

6. "I'm always punctual and I never miss a deadline."

7. "My clients know that they can count on me to get the job done."

8. "I have a proven track record of being a dependable and reliable person."

9. "I'm known for being someone who can be counted on in any situation."

10. "My clients know that they can always rely on me to deliver on my promises."

Power Phrases about Decision Making Skills

1. "I have a reputation for being a decisive and effective decision maker."

2. "I'm known for being able to make difficult decisions quickly and efficiently."

3. "My clients always appreciate my ability to make quick decisions."

4. "I'm always able to find the best solution by weighing all of the options."

5. "I have a proven track record of success in making difficult decisions."

6. "I'm known for being able to think on my feet and make quick decisions."

7. "I always make sure that I have all of the facts before making a decision."

8. "I'm known for being a very deliberate and thoughtful decision maker."

9. "I always take the time to consider all of the options before making a decision."

10. "I'm known for being a very logical and methodical decision maker."

Power Phrases about Delegating Skills

1. "I have a proven track record of being an effective delegator."

2. "My clients always appreciate my ability to delegate tasks efficiently."

3. "I'm always able to find the right person for the job."

4. "I'm known for being able to delegate effectively and get the best results."

5. "I have a knack for knowing who is best suited for each task."

6. "I'm always able to get the most out of each team member by delegating effectively."

7. "My clients know that they can count on me to delegate tasks efficiently."

8. "I'm known for being an expert at delegation and I always get great results."

9. "I always make sure that each team member is able to contribute their best by delegating effectively."

10. "My clients know that they can rely on me to get the job done by delegating tasks efficiently."

Power Phrases about Ethics

1. "I always make sure that I act in an ethical and responsible manner."

2. "My clients know that they can trust me to always do the right thing."

3. "I have a reputation for being a very honest and ethical person."

4. "I'm known for being someone who always follows the rules."

5. "I always make sure that I adhere to the highest ethical standards."

6. "My clients appreciate my commitment to acting in an ethical manner."

7. "I'm known for being a highly principled person."

8. "I always make sure that my actions are in line with my values."

9. "I'm known for being someone who is always honest and trustworthy."

10. "My clients know that they can rely on me to always act in an ethical and responsible manner."

Power Phrases about Equal Opportunity

1. "I'm committed to ensuring that everyone has an equal opportunity."

2. "I always make sure that I treat everyone fairly and equally."

3. "My clients know that they can trust me to always act in an equitable manner."

4. "I have a reputation for being a very just and unbiased person."

5. "I'm known for being someone who always follows the rules."

6. "I'm known for being a highly principled person."

7. "I always make sure that my actions are in line with my values."

8. "I always make sure that I give everyone a fair chance."

9. "I'm known for being an equal opportunity employer."

10. "My clients know that they can rely on me to always act in an ethical and responsible manner."

Power Phrases about Financial Skills

1. "I have a proven track record of being an effective financial manager."

2. "My clients always appreciate my ability to save them money."

3. "I'm known for being able to find creative solutions to financial problems."

4. "I have a reputation for being a very thrifty and resourceful person."

5. "I'm known for being able to stick to a budget."

6. "My clients know that they can rely on me to be financially responsible."

7. "I always make sure that I use resources in a wise and efficient manner."

8. "I'm known for being a very cautious and conservative spender."

9. "I have a reputation for being a very savvy investor."

10. "My clients know that they can count on me to manage their finances in a responsible and effective manner."

Power Phrases about Flexibility

1. "I'm known for being a very flexible and adaptable person."

2. "I always make sure that I'm able to adjust to any situation."

3. "My clients appreciate my ability to be flexible and accommodating."

4. "I'm known for being able to change plans at a moment's notice."

5. "I always make sure that I'm prepared for anything."

6. "I'm known for being able to think on my feet and adjust to any situation."

7. "I have a reputation for being a very flexible person."

8. "My clients know that they can count on me to be flexible and accommodating."

9. "I'm always able to make the necessary changes to get the job done."

10. "My clients know that they can rely on me to be flexible and adaptable in any situation."

Power Phrases about Forward Thinking

1. "I'm always looking for new and innovative ways to improve my work."

2. "I have a reputation for being a very forward-thinking person."

3. "My clients know that they can count on me to be on the cutting edge."

4. "I'm known for being able to think outside the box."

5. "I always make sure that I stay ahead of the curve."

6. "My clients appreciate my ability to see the big picture."

7. "I'm known for being able to think long-term and plan accordingly."

8. "I have a reputation for being a very strategic thinker."

9. "My clients know that they can rely on me to take a proactive approach."

10. "My clients know that they can count on me to be a forward-thinking and innovative thinker."

Power Phrases about Initiative

1. "I'm known for being a very proactive and self-motivated person."

2. "I always make sure that I take the initiative to get things done."

3. "My clients know that they can count on me to be a self-starter."

4. "I have a reputation for being a very go-getter."

5. "I'm always looking for new and better ways to do things."

6. "My clients appreciate my ability to think outside the box."

7. "I have a reputation for being a very resourceful person."

8. "I'm known for being able to work independently."

9. "My clients know that they can rely on me to take initiative and get the job done."

10. "My clients know that they can count on me to be a proactive and self-motivated thinker."

Power Phrases about Interpersonal Skills

1. "I'm known for being a very personable and likable person."

2. "I always make sure that I'm able to build rapport with everyone I meet."

3. "My clients appreciate my ability to relate to them."

4. "I have a reputation for being a very easygoing person."

5. "I'm always looking for ways to connect with people."

6. "My clients know that they can rely on me to be a good communicator."

7. "I'm known for being a very likable and approachable person."

8. "My clients appreciate my ability to build relationships."

9. "I'm always looking for ways to connect with people on a personal level."

10. "My clients know that they can count on me to be a great communicator and rapport builder."

Power Phrases about Innovation

1. "I'm always looking for new and innovative ways to improve my work."

2. "I have a reputation for being a very creative thinker."

3. "My clients know that they can count on me to be on the cutting edge."

4. "I'm known for being able to think outside the box."

5. "I always make sure that I stay ahead of the curve."

6. "My clients appreciate my ability to see the big picture."

7. "I'm known for being able to think long-term and plan accordingly."

8. "My clients know that they can rely on me to take a proactive approach."

9. "My clients know that they can count on me to be a forward-thinking and innovative thinker."

10. "My clients know that they can count on me to bring new and fresh ideas to the table."

Power Phrases about Job Knowledge

1. "I'm known for being a very knowledgeable person."

2. "I always make sure that I'm up-to-date on the latest industry trends."

3. "My clients know that they can count on me to be an expert in my field."

4. "I have a reputation for being a very well-informed person."

5. "I'm always looking for ways to increase my knowledge."

6. "My clients appreciate my willingness to learn new things."

7. "I have a reputation for being a very inquisitive person."

8. "My clients know that they can rely on me to be a resource of information."

9. "I'm always looking for ways to expand my knowledge base."

10. "My clients know that they can count on me to be a knowledgeable and well-informed thinker."

Power Phrases about Leadership

1. "I have a proven track record of being an effective leader."

2. "I'm known for being able to inspire and motivate others."

3. "My clients always appreciate my ability to take charge and get things done."

4. "I'm known for being a very decisive and assertive person."

5. "I always make sure that I take the lead and get things moving."

6. "My clients know that they can count on me to be a strong and effective leader."

7. "I have a reputation for being a very inspiring and motivating leader."

8. "My clients know that they can rely on me to get things done."

9. "I'm always able to take charge and get the job done."

10. "My clients know that they can count on me to be a strong and decisive leader."

Power Phrases about Management

1. "I have a proven track record of being an effective manager."

2. "I'm known for being able to lead and direct others."

3. "My clients always appreciate my ability to take charge and get things done."

4. "I'm known for being a very decisive and assertive person."

5. "I always make sure that I take the lead and get things moving."

6. "My clients know that they can count on me to be a strong and effective manager."

7. "I have a reputation for being a very inspiring and motivating manager."

8. "My clients know that they can rely on me to get things done."

9. "I'm always able to take charge and get the job done."

10. "My clients know that they can count on me to be a strong and decisive manager."

Power Phrases about Negotiation

1. "I'm known for being a very effective negotiator."

2. "My clients always appreciate my ability to find the best possible solution."

3. "I have a reputation for being a very reasonable and level-headed person."

4. "I'm always looking for ways to come to a win-win solution."

5. "My clients know that they can count on me to be a great negotiator."

6. "I'm known for being able to find creative solutions to problems."

7. "My clients know that they can rely on me to be a fair and reasonable thinker."

8. "I'm always looking for ways to reach an agreement that is beneficial for all parties

Power Phrases about Planning

1. "I'm known for being a very organized and detail-oriented person."

2. "My clients always appreciate my ability to plan ahead."

3. "I have a reputation for being a very efficient and effective planner."

4. "I'm always looking for ways to streamline and optimize my work."

5. "My clients know that they can count on me to be a great planner."

6. "I'm known for being able to think ahead and anticipate needs."

7. "My clients know that they can rely on me to be a very detail-oriented thinker."

8. "I'm always looking for ways to improve my planning and organizational skills."

9. "My clients know that they can count on me to be a great planner and thinker."

10. "I'm always looking for ways to optimize and streamline my work."

Power Phrases about Presentation Skills

1. "I'm known for being a very effective presenter."

2. "My clients always appreciate my ability to deliver clear and concise presentations."

3. "I have a reputation for being a very articulate and well-spoken person."

4. "I'm always looking for ways to improve my presentation skills."

5. "My clients know that they can count on me to be a great presenter."

6. "I'm known for being able to deliver engaging and informative presentations."

7. "My clients know that they can rely on me to be a very clear and concise speaker."

8. "I'm always looking for ways to make my presentations more interesting and engaging."

9. "My clients know that they can count on me to be a great presenter and speaker."

10. "I'm always looking for ways to improve my presentation skills."

Power Phrases about Problem Solving

1. "I'm known for being a very resourceful person."

2. "I always make sure that I find creative solutions to problems."

3. "My clients know that they can count on me to be a quick thinker."

4. "I'm known for being able to think on my feet."

5. "I always make sure that I'm prepared for anything."

6. "My clients appreciate my ability to find innovative solutions."

7. "I have a reputation for being a very adaptable and resourceful thinker."

8. "My clients know that they can rely on me to be a creative problem solver."

9. "I'm always looking for new and better ways to solve problems."

10. "My clients know that they can count on me to be a resourceful and adaptable thinker."

Power Phrases about Results-Oriented

1. "I'm known for being a very results-oriented person."

2. "I always make sure that I get the job done."

3. "My clients appreciate my ability to produce results."

4. "I have a reputation for being a very driven person."

5. "I'm always looking for ways to improve my work and get better results."

6. "My clients know that they can rely on me to get the job done."

7. "I'm known for being a very hard worker."

8. "My clients appreciate my dedication to my work."

9. "I'm always looking for ways to go above and beyond."

10. "My clients know that they can count on me to produce results."

Power Phrases about Responsibility

1. "I'm known for being a very responsible person."

2. "I always make sure that I'm able to take care of everything I need to."

3. "My clients know that they can rely on me to be responsible."

4. "I have a reputation for being a very dependable person."

5. "I'm always looking for ways to be more responsible."

6. "My clients appreciate my ability to take care of everything."

7. "I'm known for being a very reliable person."

8. "My clients know that they can count on me to be dependable."

9. "I always make sure that I'm able to handle everything in a responsible manner."

10. "My clients know that they can count on me to be a responsible and dependable thinker."

Power Phrases about Strategic Thinking

1. "I'm known for being a very strategic thinker."

2. "I always make sure that I'm thinking ahead."

3. "My clients know that they can rely on me to think strategically."

4. "I have a reputation for being a very detail-oriented person."

5. "I'm always looking for ways to improve my work and get better results."

6. "My clients appreciate my ability to think ahead."

7. "I'm known for being a very forward-thinking person."

8. "My clients know that they can count on me to be proactive."

9. "I'm always looking for ways to plan ahead."

10. "My clients know that they can count on me to be a strategic thinker."

Power Phrases about Team Building

1. "I'm known for building vibrant teams with diverse individuals pulling in the same direction."

2. "I always make sure that I'm working well with others and this reflects in my team."

3. "My clients know that they can rely on me to be a team player."

4. "I have a reputation for being a very cooperative person."

5. "I'm always looking for ways to improve my team's performance."

6. "My clients appreciate my ability to build strong teams."

7. "I'm known for being a very collaborative person."

8. "My clients know that they can count on me to be a team player."

9. "I always make sure that I'm working well with others."

10. "My clients know that they can count on me to build strong and successful teams."

Power Phrases about Time Management

1. "My clients know that they can count on me to manage my time effectively."

2. "I'm very efficient in my work and I always make sure that projects are completed on time."

3. "I have a reputation for being a very organized and efficient person."

4. "I'm known for being able to get the most out of each day."

5. "I always make sure that I use my time wisely."

6. "My clients appreciate my ability to always stay on schedule."

7. "I'm always willing to put in the extra work to make sure that projects are completed on time."

8. "I always make sure that I prioritize my tasks in an effective manner."

9. "I'm known to be a very detail-oriented person who always stays on top of things."

10. "My clients know that they can count on me to always deliver on time."

Power Phrases about Training and Development

1. "I'm passionate about training and development and I always make sure that I'm up-to-date on the latest trends."

2. "I have a reputation for being a very knowledgeable person."

3. "I'm known for being able to train others effectively."

4. "I have a lot of experience in training and development."

5. "I'm known for being able to share my knowledge with others."

6. "My clients appreciate my ability to train them effectively."

7. "I'm always looking for ways to improve my skills and knowledge."

8. "I'm known for being a lifelong learner."

9. "I'm always willing to invest in my own development."

10. "My clients know that they can count on me for training and development."

Power Phrases about Writing

1. "I have a reputation for being a very articulate writer."

2. "I'm known for being able to communicate effectively in writing."

3. "I have a lot of experience in writing and I always make sure that my work is of the highest quality."

4. "I'm known for being a very detail-oriented writer."

5. "I always make sure that my work is clear and concise."

6. "My clients appreciate my ability to communicate effectively in writing."

7. "I'm always looking for ways to improve my writing skills."

8. "I'm known for being a very effective and efficient writer."

9. "I always make sure that my work is of the highest quality."

10. "My clients know that they can count on me for excellent writing."

Power Phrases about Quality of Work

1. "I always make sure that I produce high-quality work."

2. "My clients know that they can count on me to deliver quality results."

3. "I'm known for paying attention to the details and making sure that everything is perfect."

4. "I have a reputation for being a very detail-oriented person."

5. "I'm always looking for ways to improve my work and make it the best it can be."

6. "My clients appreciate my dedication to quality."

7. "I'm known for being a very quality-focused individual."

8. "My clients know that they can count on me to produce high-quality work."

9. "I always make sure that I'm meeting or exceeding my clients' expectations."

10. "My clients know that they can count on me to deliver quality results every time."

Power Phrases about Work Ethic

1. "I have a strong work ethic."

2. "My clients know that they can count on me to work hard."

3. "I'm always looking for ways to improve my work and get better results."

4. "I have a reputation for being a very dedicated and hardworking person."

5. "I'm known for being a very dependable and hardworking individual."

6. "My clients appreciate my dedication to my work."

7. "I always make sure that I'm putting in the extra effort."

8. "I'm known for going above and beyond what's expected."

9. "My clients know that they can count on me to always give 100%."

10. "I'm a very hard worker and I always make sure that my work is of the highest quality."

Power Phrases about Work Habits

1. "I have a reputation for being a very reliable and consistent worker."

2. "My clients know that they can count on me to be a consistent performer."

3. "I'm known for always meeting my deadlines."

4. "I'm always looking for ways to improve my work habits."

5. "I have a reputation for being a very detail-oriented and organized person."

6. "My clients appreciate my ability to always stay on top of things."

7. "I'm known to be a very punctual and reliable person."

8. "My clients know that they can count on me to always be there when they need me."

9. "I'm a very dependable person and my clients know that they can always count on me."

10. "I'm known for being a very responsible and reliable worker."

Conclusion

These are just a few examples, but feel free to use your own power verbs and phrases that you think will help you stand out to potential employers!

We hope you will use this book to gain an advance in your job search and get your resume noticed. Please remember to leave a review online about your job search and help others find this book.